DANIEL THE MAN OF GOD

By

DR. EMMA T. WARREN

First Edition

©January 2018

Bibliography: James Orr M.A., D.D. General Editor International Standard Bible Encyclopedia, Matthew Henry's Commentary On the whole Bible Publishers, Hendrickson, the Nelson's Illustrated Bible Dictionary Thomas Nelson Publishers 1968, Old Testament Survey Second Edition William B. Eerdmans Publishing Company First Edition 1982, Second Edition 1996.

Publish by

**2260 South Ferdon Blvd Suite 110
Crestview, FL 32536**

For Worldwide Distribution
This book printed in the U. S. A.

ISBN-13: 978-1983983603
ISBN 10: 1983983608

To reach us on the Internet:
Web Site: http://www.dretwc.com

ACKNOWLEDGMENTS

Guided by God the Father, God the Son and God the Holy Spirit; and the encouragement and support of many people for this book has been a source of inspiration and I would like to offer my sincere gratitude for all the understanding and kindness I received.

Emma wishes to express her sincere appreciation to the intercessor Zarlee Dillon for her support, prayers, patience, and participation helping to make this book possible. In addition, special thanks to the professors and teachers whose familiarity with the needs and ideas of the research was helpful during the class in the early programming phase of this undertaking.

With a grateful heart, I would like to give special thanks to Allan Parker of The Justice Foundation, Alice Patterson of the Justice at the Gate and Cathe Halford at Pray Texas, for the act of acknowledging and helping to move me into the prophetic call and being an example that lead me into writing this book.

Dr. Emma T Warren
DRETWC Ministries
Crestview FL 32536

DEDICATED TO THE READERS

"Blessed Lord, who hast cause all Holy Scriptures to be for our learning; Grant that we may in such wise hear them, read them, mark them, learn and inwardly digest them, that by patience and comfort of the Holy Word, we may embrace, and ever hold fast, the blessed hope of everlasting life, which is given to us in our Savior, Jesus Christ.

For it is the Spirit that quickened; the flesh profited nothing: the words that I speak unto you, they are Spirit and they are life." As the power of our God goes into motion it begins through the confession of God's promises for whatever situation, circumstance, or need you to have. As we begin to confess God's Word, a very powerful spiritual principle goes to work in the lives of those who are hearing, reading and reaping the benefit of it.

The Author would like to give thanks to all who read this publication, because, it is dedicated to you; by the grace of God, it is the prayers that the words of God in this publication will bless you, heal you and make you free moving you forward on your journey with Christ and in Christ. May the God of our salvation grant you the wisdom, knowledge, understanding and the Revelation of his word and who He truly is; blessings to you all.

INTERDICTION

As we are passing through times on our journey in this life we need hope and by the Grace of God we need the gift of prayer and to be intercessors more than ever before because of the times we live in. Daniel knew that prayer was the only thing that could solve the problems that he had with the men that were plotting against him. Look at what is happening today with our government. The greed and hunger for power have nearly overtaken this great nation of our; corruption in our government is on every side, our leader is undoing everything that is good for the people out of pure wackiness.

Daniel the chosen man of God a prophet in the times of King Nebuchadnezzar and Cyrus the hero and author of the Book of Daniel doing the times of Nebuchadnezzar kingdom. We know nothing of the early life of Daniel, except what is recorded in the book bearing his name. Here it is said that he was one of the youths of royal or noble seed, Daniel by which were carried captive by Nebuchadnezzar in the third year of Jehoiakim the king of Judah. These youths were without blemish, well-favored; skillful in all wisdom, endued with knowledge, and understanding science, and such as had ability to stand in the king's palace.

The king commanded to teach them the knowledge and tongue of the Chaldeans and appointed for them a daily portion of the king's food and of the wine which he drank. After having been nourished for three years, they were to stand before the king. Ashpenaz, the master or chief of the eunuchs, into whose hands they had been entrusted, following a custom of the time, gave to each of these youths a new and Babylonian name.

The youth after being hostage of Jehoiakim at the court of the king of Babylon came to the kingdom of King Nebuchadnezzar. The youths were probably from 12 to 15 years of age at the time when they were carried captive.

Daniel's public activities were in harmony with his education. His first appearance was as an interpreter of the dream recorded in Dan 2 Nebuchadnezzar having seen in his dream a vision of a great image, excellent in brightness and terrible in appearance, its head of fine gold, its breast and its arms of silver, its belly and its thighs of brass, its legs of iron, its feet part of iron and part of clay, beheld a stone cut out without hands smiting the image and breaking it in pieces, until it became like chaff and was carried away by the wind; while the stone that smote the image became a great mountain and filled the whole earth.

When the king awoke from his troubled sleep, he forgot, or reigned that he had forgotten, the dream, and summoned the wise men of Babylon both to tell him the dream and to give the interpretation thereof. The wise men have said that they could not tell the dream, nor interpret it as long as it was untold, the king threatened them with death. The wise men were left without words and full of fear for their lives. They knew that the King was troubled, and that was not good.

Daniel, who seems not to have been present when the otherwise men were before the king, when he was informed of the threat of the king, and that preparations were being made to slay all of the wise men of Babylon, himself and his three companions included, boldly went in to the king and requested that he would appoint a time for him to appear to show the interpretation, Then he went to his house, and he and his companions prayed, and the dream and its interpretation were made known unto Daniel.

Daniel's third great appearance in the book is in chapter 5 where he is called upon to explain the extraordinary writing upon the wall of King Belshazzar's palace, which foretold the end of the Babylonian empire and the incoming of the Medes and Persians. For this service Daniel was clothed with purple, a chain of gold put around his neck, and he was made the third ruler in the kingdom.

Daniel, however, was not merely an interpreter of other men's visions. In the last six chapters, we have recorded four or five of his own visions, all of which are taken up with revelations concerning the future history of the great world empires, especially in their relation to the people of God, and predictions of the final triumph of the Messiah's kingdom. In addition to his duties as a seer and as an interpreter of signs and dreams, Daniel also stood high in the governmental service of Nebuchadnezzar, Belshazzar, and Darius the Mede, and perhaps also of Cyrus.

In all of these positions, he seems to have conducted himself with faithfulness and judgment. While in the service of Darius the Mede, he aroused the antipathy of the other presidents and of the satraps. Unable to find any fault with his official acts, they induced the king to make a decree, apparently general in form and purpose, but really aimed at Daniel alone. They saw that they could find no valid accusation against him unless they found it in connection with something concerning the law of his God.

They, therefore, caused the king to make a decree that no one should make a request of anyone for the space of thirty days, save of the king. Daniel, having publicly prayed three times a day as he was in the habit of doing, was caught in the act, accused, and on account of the irrevocability of a law of the Medes and Persians, was condemned in accordance with the decree to be cast into a den of lions. The king was much troubled at this but was unable to withhold the punishment. However, he expressed to Daniel his belief that his God in whom he trusted continually would deliver him; and so indeed it came to pass. For in the morning, when the king drew near to the mouth of the den and called to him, Daniel said that God had sent His angel and shut the mouths of the lions. Daniel was taken up unharmed, and at the command of the king his accusers, having been cast into tile den, were destroyed before they reached the bottom.

ABSTRACT

Christ-Cantered Relationship

Focuses on who Christ is, what He has done for us in His life, death, resurrection and in sending the Holy Spirit. Christ-centered focuses on what He is doing for us right now in His intercession at the Father's right hand, and what He will yet do for us in the future.

The Christ of the Bible is not an appendage or a "tack on" for living in the fast lane. Rather, He is at the center as well as the circumference, and everywhere in between. Christ-centered involves understanding the nature and causes of our human difficulties.

It involves understanding the ways we are unlike Christ: like in our values, aspirations, desires, thoughts, feelings, choices, attitudes, actions, and responses. Resolving those sin-related difficulties includes being redeemed and justified through Christ, receiving God's forgiveness through Christ, and acquiring from Christ the enabling power to replace un-Christ-like (sinful) patterns of life with Christ-like, Godly ones.

Salvation-Centered Understanding: To have the change for beliefs to become more agreeable within our conscience and including their understanding in his or her outlook on life. Truly done by individuals who will experience the regenerating work of the Holy Spirit, and will come to Christ in repentance and faith, acknowledging Him as Lord and Savior of their lives. These are also people who want to live in obedience to Him; people whose main concern in life is to exalt Him and bring glory to His name. They are people who believe that, since God did not spare His own Son (from and on the cross) but delivered Him up (to the cross and death) for us (on our behalf and in our stead, as our substitute).

He will freely through Christ give us all that we need for effective and productive living (for transforming us into the very likeness of His Son in the totality of our being). With Biblical understanding, we also acknowledge the role of the Holy Spirit in regenerating, saving, and sanctifying the believer. The new theological will convictions influence, permeate and control our personal lives and practice.

Bible-Centered Changes: Truly based on the Bible, deriving its understanding of which man is the nature of his main problems, why he has these problems, and how to resolve these problems from Scripture. In other words, he or she must be committed to the sufficiency of Scripture for understanding and resolving all the nonphysical personal and interpersonal sin-related difficulties of man and woman in life.

Church-Centered Teachings: Another distinguishing feature of truly understand the sins of the fathers are that it will be church-centered. Scripture makes it clear that the local church is the primary means by which God accomplishes His work in the world as His foundation. For the believer, the local church is His ordained instrument for calling the lost to

Himself and the context in which He sanctifies and changes His people into the very likeness of Christ.

According to Scripture, the church is His household, the pillar, and support of the truth, and the instrument He uses in helping His people to put off the old manner of life and to put on the new self. (1Timothy 3:15)

But if I should delay, that you may know how you ought to behave in the house of God, which is the church of the living God, the pillar and foundation of the truth.

Ephesians 4:1-32

The Biblical God-given truth which is eternal and unchangeable in contrast to biblical "truth" of psychology is every changing and contradictory by men. Therefore, biblical teaching is more effective than secular teaching in which there is an attempt to integrate the psychology of men with the Scriptures. The only way is God's way.

TABLE OF CONTENTS

DANIEL the MAN of GOD

THE SEER
THE DREAMER
THE INTERPRETER
THE WRITER
And
God's Prophet

DR. EMMA T. WARREN

© **January 2018**

Chapter 1

Daniel

all wisdom, endued with knowledge, and understanding science, and such as had ability to stand in the king's palace.

The king commanded to teach Daniel and the other boys the knowledge and tongue of the Chaldeans and appointed for them a daily portion of the king's food and of the wine which he drank. Daniel belongs to a genre of literature known as apocalyptic. Through story and vision, it communicates the most mysterious massage of the Old Testament: the kingdoms of this world are not beyond God's control; in fact, they one day will be replaced by God' own kingdom.

Daniel gives glimpses of the future. In the text of Daniel, however, this massage is sustained despite the arrogance of the world empire. It is revealed in visions that convey the passionate intent of God to reign as sovereign over his creation.

It seems pitiful that a work of such grandeur has sometimes been ridiculed as the record of fantasies of people too much oppressed or used merely as the vehicle for speculation about the end of the world and setting of dates for end-time events. Better to grasp the colossal promise of God who governs world history that to design caricatures that belittle this noble prospect.

And in the days of these kings, the God of Heaven shall set up a kingdom which shall never be destroyed. And the kingdom shall not be left to other peoples, but it shall crush and destroy all these kingdoms, and it shall stand forever.
(Daniel 2:44)

Daniel is, however, a very different kind of prophecy from that of most of the prophets. As indicated, the purpose of the prophets of Israel was to make known Yahweh's willed, including the future of the world.

Even in their punishment, the people of God were to cherish the hope of their restoration. So, the dimension of foretelling is present in all of the prophetic tradition, even when it is secondary to God's call to covenant obedience, God's ultimate purpose (teleology), Daniel's main theme, was and is always a part of the full meaning of Israel's prophecy.

In the apocalyptic prophecy, the stress is clearly in the future. The book of Daniel begins in the Babylonian court and recounts the action of Babylonian or Persian kings. His visions there include Persian, Greece, and kings of the north and south, rulers that make trouble for the people of God, an anointed one cut off, and the cessation of sacrifices.

The readers seem encouraged to fit these prophecies into real historical situations. As the people of God, they are then both comforted in a historical need (as the stories stress) and pointed to a future bound up with God, a future displayed especially in the visions.

Apocalyptic prophecy is given in forms that are to be understood as both timely and timeless. Knowledge of the time of the end is sealed up, but the people of God are called into circumstances where they ask, as did Daniel: "How long shall it be till the end of these wonders?" "What shall be the outcome of these things?" (12:6, 8).

The message is perseverance and hope. Only when one loses a grip upon this purpose and attempts to unseal the book or to fit apocalyptic visions into historical schemes (or vice versa), does the primary message become obscure? The book of Daniel was never intended to exhaust its meaning in the days of Antiochus Epiphanies (175-164 B.C.) or the Roman destruction of Jerusalem, in A.D. 70, or in any calamity the world has yet known.

It was intended "for the time of the end," and, for as long as time last to proclaim to all who believe that their times are in God's hands, even in the midst of persecution. The twofold truth that Daniel announces is (1) the highest rules, and (2) his saints will one day inherit a kingdom which shall never be destroyed.

The Early Life of Daniel:

We know nothing of the early life of Daniel, except what is recorded in the book bearing his name. Here it is said that he was one of the youths of royal or noble seed, which were carried captive by Nebuchadnezzar in the third year of Jehoiakim, king of Judah. These youths were without blemish, well-favored; skillful in After having been nourished for three years, they were to stand before the king. Ashpenaz, the master or chief of the eunuchs, into whose hands they had been entrusted, following a custom of the time, gave to each of these youths a new and Babylonian name. To Daniel, he gave the name Belshazzar. In Babylonian this name was probably Belu-Lita-Sharri-user, which means "O Bel, protect thou the hostage of the king," a most appropriate name for one in the place which Daniel occupied as a hostage of Jehoiakim at the court of the king of Babylon. The youths were probably from 12 to 15 years of age at the time when they were carried captive.

Having purposed in his heart that he would not defile himself with the food and drink of the king, Daniel requested of Ashpenaz permission to eat vegetables and drink water.

Through the favor of God, this request was granted, notwithstanding the fear of Ashpenaz that his head would be endangered to the king on account of the probably resulting from the poor appearance of the youths living upon this blood-diluting diet, in comparison with the expected healthy appearance of the others of their class. However, ten days' trial having been first granted, and at the end of that time their countenances having been found fairer and their flesh fatter than the other youths', the permission was made permanent. God gave to Daniel and his companion's knowledge and skill in all learning and wisdom, and to Daniel understanding in all visions and dreams; so that at the end of the three years when the king communed with them, he found them much superior to all the magicians and enchanters in every matter of wisdom and understanding.

Daniel the Dream Interpreter:

Daniel's public activities were in harmony with his education. His first appearance was as an interpreter of the dream recorded in Dan 2. Nebuchadnezzar had seen in his dream a vision of a great image, excellent in brightness and terrible in appearance, its head of fine gold, its breast and its arms of silver, its belly and its thighs of brass, its legs of iron, its feet part of iron and part of clay, beheld a stone cut out without hands smiting the image and breaking it in pieces, until it became like chaff and was carried away by the wind.

While the stone that smote the image became a great mountain and filled the whole earth. When the king awoke from his troubled sleep, he forgot, or reigned that he had forgotten, the dream, and summoned the wise men of Babylon both to tell him the dream and to give the interpretation thereof. The wise men have said that they could not tell the dream, nor interpret it as long as it was untold, the king threatened them with death.

Daniel, who seems not to have been present when the otherwise men were before the king, when he was informed of the threat of the king, and that preparations were being made to slay all of the wise men of Babylon, himself and his three companions included, boldly went in to the king and requested that he would appoint a time for him to appear to show the interpretation, Then he went to his house, and he and his companions prayed, and the dream and its interpretation were made known unto Daniel.

At the appointed time, the dream was explained and the four Hebrew's were loaded with wealth and given high positions in the service of the king. In the 4th chapter, we have recorded Daniel's interpretation of the dream of Nebuchadnezzar about the great tree that was hewn at the command of an angel, prefiguring the insanity of the king.

Daniel the interpreter of signs:

Daniel's third great appearance in the book is in chapter 5 where he is called upon to explain the extraordinary writing upon the wall of Belshazzar's palace, which foretold the end of the Babylonian empire and the incoming of the Medes and Persians. For this service Daniel was clothed with purple, a chain of gold put around his neck, and he was made the third ruler in the kingdom.

Chapter 2

Daniel and the King

The greatest men are most open to cares and troubles of mind, which disturb their repose in the night, while the sleep of the laboring man is sweet and sound. We know not the uneasiness of many who live in great pomp, and, as others vainly think, in pleasure also. The king said that his learned men must tell him the dream itself, or they should all be put to death as deceivers.

Men are more eager to ask as to future events than to learn the way of salvation or the path of duty, yet foreknowledge of future events increases anxiety and trouble. Those who deceived, by pretending to do what they could not do, were sentenced to death, for not being able to do what they did not pretend to.

Daniel humbly prayed that God would discover to him the king's dream and the meaning of it. Praying friends are valuable friends, and it well becomes the greatest and best men to desire the prayers of others. Let us show that we value our friends and their prayers. They were particular in prayer. And whatever we pray for, we can expect nothing but as the gift of God's mercies.

God gives us leave in prayer to tell our wants and burdens. Their plea with God was the peril they were in. The mercy Daniel and his fellows prayed for was bestowed. The fervent prayers of righteous men avail much. Daniel was thankful to God for making known that to him, which saved the lives of himself and his fellows. How much more should we be thankful to God, for making known the great salvation of the soul to those who are not among the worldly-wise and prudent!

Daniel takes away the king's opinion of his magicians and soothsayers. The insufficiency of creatures should drive us to the all-sufficiency of the Creator. There is one who can do that for us, and make known that to us, which none on earth can, particularly the work of redemption, and the secret designs of God's love to us that believe.

Daniel confirmed the king in his opinion, that the dream was of great consequence, relating to the affairs and changes of this lower world. Let those whom God has highly favored and honored, lays aside all opinion of their own wisdom and worthiness, that the Lord alone may be praised for the good they have and do.

Daniel answered before the king and said the secret which the king has demanded cannot be shown to the king by the wise men, the conjurers, the horoscopes, or the fortune-tellers. But there is a God in Heaven who reveals secrets and makes known to King Nebuchadnezzar what shall be in the latter days. Your dream and the visions of your head upon your bed are these.

(Dan 2:27-28)

This image represented the kingdoms of the earth that should successively rule the nations and influence the affairs of the Jewish church.

The head of gold signified the Chaldean empire, then in being. The breast and arms of silver signified the empire of the Medes and Persians. The belly and thighs of brass signified the Grecian empire, founded by Alexander. The legs and feet of iron signified the Roman Empire.

The Roman Empire branched into ten kingdoms, as the toes of these feet. Some were weak as clay, others strong as iron. Endeavors have often been used to unite them, for strengthening the empire, but in vain. The stone cut out without hands, represented the kingdom of our Lord Jesus Christ, which should be set up in the kingdoms of the world, upon the ruins of Satan's kingdom in them.

This was the Stone which the builders refused because it was not cut out by their hands, but it becomes the headstone of the corner. Of the increase of Christ's government and peace, there shall be no end.

The Lord shall reign, not only to the end of time but when time and days shall be no more. As far as events have gone, the fulfilling this prophetic vision has been most exact and undeniable; future ages shall witness this Stone destroying the image and filling the whole earth.

Then King Nebuchadnezzar fell on his face and worshiped Daniel, and he commanded to offer an offering and incense to him.

(Daniel 2:46)

<u>Daniel Promotion by the King:</u>

The king answered Daniel and said it is true that your God *is* a God of gods, and a Lord of kings, and a revealer of secrets since you could reveal this secret. Then the king made Daniel great, and gave him many great gifts, and made him ruler over all the province of Babylon and chief of the perfects over all the wise men of Babylon.

And Daniel asked the king, and he set Shadrach, Meshach, and Abednego over the affairs of the province of Babylon. But Daniel sat in the gate of the king. God's favor is like no other. What a mighty God we serve. There is a favorite when you trust God and stand in faith.

<u>Daniel Friends Trust God:</u>

True devotion calms the spirit, quiets and softens it, but superstition and devotion to false gods inflame men's passions. The matter is put into a little compass, Turn, or burn. Proud men are still ready to say, like Nebuchadnezzar, who is the Lord, that I should fear his power? Shadrach, Meshach, and Abednego did not hesitate whether they should comply or not. Life or death was not to be considered.

Those that would avoid sin must not parley with temptation when that to which we are allured or affrighted is manifestly evil. Stand not to pause about it, but say, as Christ did get thee behind me, Satan. They did not contrive an evasive answer when a direct answer was expected.

Those who make their duty their main care need not be anxious or fearful concerning the event. The faithful servants of God find him able to control and overrule all the powers armed against them. Lord, if thou wilt, thou canst. If He is for us, we need not fear what man can do unto us. God will deliver us, either from death or in death. They must obey God rather than man; they must rather suffer than sin, and must not do evil that good may come. Therefore, none of these things moved them.

The saving them from sinful compliance, was as great a miracle in the kingdom of grace, as the saving them out of the fiery furnace was in the kingdom of nature. Fear of man and love of the world; especially want of faith, make men yield to temptation, while a firm persuasion of the truth will deliver them from denying Christ, or being ashamed of him. We are to be meek in our replies, but we must be decided that we will obey God rather than man.

Let Nebuchadnezzar heat his furnace as hot as he can, a few minutes will finish the torment of those cast into it, but hell-fire tortures, and yet does not kill. Those who worshipped the beast and his image have no rest, no pause, no moment free from pain, (*Rev 14:10, Rev 14:1)1.*

Now was fulfilled in the letter that great promise, *Isa 43:2,* when thou walk through the fire, thou shall not be burned. Leaving it to that God who preserved them in the fire, to bring them out, they walked up and down in the midst, supported and encouraged by the presence of the Son of God. Those who suffer for Christ, have his presence in their sufferings, even in the fiery furnace, and in the valley of the shadow of death.

Those who suffer for Christ, have his presence in their sufferings, even in the fiery furnace, and in the valley of the shadow of death. Nebuchadnezzar owns them for servants of the highest God; a God able to deliver them out of his hand. It is our God only is the consuming fire, (Hebrews 12:29). Could we but see into the eternal world, we should behold the persecuted believer safe from the malice of his foes, while they are exposed to the wrath of God, and tormented in unquenchable fires.

I, King Nebuchadnezzar, have seen this dream. Now you, O Belshazzar, declare its meaning, because all the wise men of my kingdom are not able to make the meaning known to me. But you are able, for the spirit of the holy gods is in you.
(Daniel 4:18)

Daniel's interpretation of Nebuchadnezzar's vision; Daniel was struck with amazement and terror at so heavy a judgment coming upon so great a prince and gives advice with tenderness and respect. It is necessary, in repentance that we not only cease to do evil but learn to do well.

Though it might not wholly prevent the judgment, yet the trouble maybe longer before it comes, or shorter when it does come but know that it will come. And everlasting misery will be escaped by all who repent and turn to God.

Nebuchadnezzar's Humiliation:

"All this came on the King Nebuchadnezzar. At the end of twelve months, he walked in the palace of the kingdom of Babylon. The king spoke and said is this not great Babylon that I have built for the house of the kingdom by the might of my power and for the honor of my majesty?

While the word was in the king's mouth, a voice fell from Heaven, saying, to the king: O King Nebuchadnezzar, to you, it is spoken. The kingdom has departed from you. And they shall drive you from men, and your dwelling shall be with the animals of the field. They shall make you eat grass like oxen, and seven times shall pass over you until you know that the Highest rules in the kingdom of men, and gives it to whomever He will. The same hour the thing was fulfilled on Nebuchadnezzar. And he was driven from men and ate grass like oxen, and his body was wet with the dew of the heavens until his hair had grown like eagles' feathers, and his nails like birds' claws.

And at the end of days, I Nebuchadnezzar lifted up my eyes to Heaven, and my understanding returned to me, and I blessed the Highest, and I praised and honored Him who lives forever, whose kingdom is an everlasting kingdom, and His rule is from generation to generation. And all the people of the earth are counted as nothing, and He does according to His will in the army of heaven, and among the people of the earth. And none can strike His hand, or say to Him, what are you doing? At that time my reason returned to me. And the glory of my kingdom, my honor and brightness returned to me. And my advisers and my lords came for me, and I was established in my kingdom, and excellent majesty was added to me. Now I Nebuchadnezzar praise and exalt and honor the King of heaven, all whose works are truth and His ways judgment. And those who walk in pride He is able to humble. (Dan 4:28-37)

And at the end of days, I Nebuchadnezzar lifted up my eyes to Heaven, and my understanding returned to me, and I blessed the Highest, and I praised and honored Him who lives forever, whose kingdom is an everlasting kingdom, and His rule is from generation to generation.

And all the people of the earth are counted as nothing, and He does according to His will in the army of heaven, and among the people of the earth. And none can strike His hand, or say to Him, what are you doing?

At that time my reason returned to me. And the glory of my kingdom, my honor and brightness returned to me. And my advisers and my lords came for me, and I was established in my kingdom, and excellent majesty was added to me.

(Daniel 4:34-36)

Pride and self-conceit are sins that beset great men. They have the tendency to take that glory for them which is due to God only. While the proud word was in the king's mouth, but the powerful word came from God. His understanding and his memory were gone, and all the powers of the rational soul were broken.

How careful we ought to be, not to do anything which may provoke God to put us out of our senses! God resists the proud. Nebuchadnezzar would be more than a man, but God justly makes him less than a man. We may learn to believe concerning God, that the highest God lives forever, and that his kingdom is like himself, everlasting, and universal. His power cannot be resisted.

When men are brought to honor God, and by the sovereignty, then, and not till then, they may expect that God will honor them; not only restore them to the dignity they lost by the sin of the first Adam, but add excellent majesty to them, from the righteousness and grace of the Second Adam.

Afflictions shall last no longer than till they have done the work for which they were sent. There can be no reasonable doubt that Nebuchadnezzar was a true penitent, and an accepted believer. It is thought that he did not live more than a year after his restoration. Thus, the Lord knows how to abase those that walk in pride, but gives grace and consolation to the humble, broken-hearted sinner who calls upon Him.

Chapter 3

Daniel Trial by Fire

There are all kinds of difficulties to endure in ministry and as a servant of the lord. In Daniel, we learn how to handle the roadblocks and hurdles to the cross. But there's a trial by fire that goes beyond common problems, but to pass it is worth all the cost.

This is the trial where the issues of faith are tested like never before, where the heart has to believe what God says is true despite the circumstances and heartache that land at our door. The trial by fire teaches us how to develop a prayer life with intensity each day; to believe God is faithful through the silence we hear and that he's listening to us as we pray.

The trial by fire is an uncomfortable place God will allow us to go through for the good. In the fire comes the wisdom of heaven that we would not understand without the fire, and what it means to persevere finding ourselves stronger than we ever knew. For god sustains us and strengthens us for the mission at hand and every hard day that we're going through. We become a different person through the testing and pain with the will of God as our growing desire. I believe that we're more humble, tendered, and much stronger with the gifts of wisdom, knowledge, revelation and much more understanding. Before Daniel be was promoted by the king he had to go through the fire.

Daniel and the den of Lions:

Nebuchadnezzar, king of Babylon, in the first year of his reign, took Jerusalem and carried whom and what he pleased away. From this first captivity, most think the seventy years are to be dated. It is the interest of princes to employ wise men, and it is their wisdom to find out and train up such.

Nebuchadnezzar ordered that these chosen youths should be taught. All their Hebrew names had something of God in them; but to make them forget the God of their fathers, the guide of their youth, the heathen gave them names that savored of idolatry. It is painful to reflect how often public education tends to corrupt the principles and morals.

The interest we think we make for ourselves, we must acknowledge being God's gift. Daniel was still firm to his religion. Whatever they called him, he still held fast the spirit of an Israelite. These youths scrupled concerning the meat, lest it should be sinful. When God's people are in Babylon they need to take special care that they partake not of her sins.

It is much to the praise of young people, not to covet or seek the delights of sense. Those who would excel in wisdom and piety must learn betimes to keep the body under.

Daniel avoided defiling himself with sin, and we should more fear that than any outward trouble. It is easier to keep temptation at a distance than to resist it when near.

And we cannot better improve our interest in any with whom we have found favor than to use it to keep us from sin.

People will not believe the benefit of avoiding excess, and of a spare diet, nor how much they contribute to the health of the body unless they try. Conscientious temperance will always do more, even for the comfort of this life, than sinful indulgence.

But Daniel lay on his heart that he would not defile himself with the king's food, nor with the wine which he drank. So, he asked permission of the chief of the eunuchs that he might not defile himself.   *Daniel 1:8*

Daniel and his fellows kept to their religion, and God rewarded them with eminence in learning. Pious young persons should Endeavour to do better than their fellows in useful things; not for the praise of man, but for the honor of the gospel, and that they may be qualified for God and his usefulness.

And it is well for a country, and for the honor of a prince when he can judge who is best fitted to serve him and prefers them on that account. Let young men steadily attend to this chapter, and let all remember that God will honor those who honor him, but those who despise him shall be lightly esteemed.

"It pleased Darius to set over the kingdom a hundred and twenty satraps that they might be over the whole kingdom. And over them were three presidents (Daniel was one of them), so that these satraps might give account to them, and the king should have no loss. Then this Daniel was made overseer of the presidents and satraps because an excellent spirit was in him.

And the king was planning to set him over the entire kingdom. Then the presidents and rulers sought to find occasion against Daniel concerning the kingdom. But they could find no occasion or fault because he was faithful. Neither was there any error or fault found in him.

Then these men said we shall not find any occasion against this Daniel unless we find it against him concerning the Law of his God. Then these presidents and rulers assembled to the king and said this to him: King Darius, live forever.

All the presidents of the kingdom, the prefects, and the satraps, and the officials and governors, have planned together to establish a royal law, and to make a strong ban that whoever shall ask a petition of any god or man for thirty days, except from you, O king; he shall be thrown into the den of lions.

Now, oh king, establish the ban and sign the writing, so that it may not be changed, according to the law of the Medes and Persians which cannot be changed. Therefore, King Darius signed the writing and the ban. And when he had learned that the document was signed, Daniel went to his house. And his windows were open in his roof room toward Jerusalem; and he kneeled on his knees three times a day and prayed, and gave thanks before his God, as he did before.

Then these men assembled and found Daniel praying and confessing before his God. Then they came near and spoke before the king concerning the king's ban, have you not signed a ban that every man who shall ask a petition of any god or man within thirty days, except you, O king, shall be thrown into the lion's den? The king answered and said; the thing is true, according to the law of the Medes and Persians, which cannot be changed.

Then they answered and said before the king, Daniel, who is of the exiled sons of Judah, has not respected you, O king, or the ban that you have signed, but makes his prayer three times a day. Then the king, when he heard the word, was very much displeased with himself.

And he set his heart on Daniel to deliver him. And he labored until sundown to deliver him. Then these men met before the king and said to the king, Know, O king that the law of the Medes and Persians is not that no ban nor law which the king establishes may be changed. Then the king commanded, and they brought Daniel and threw him into the lions' den. The king answered and said to Daniel, Your God, whom you always serve, will deliver you. And a stone was brought and laid on the mouth of the den.

And the king sealed it with his own signet, and with the signet of his lords, that the purpose might not be changed concerning Daniel. Then the king went to his palace and spent the night fasting. And diversions were not brought before him, and his sleep fled from him. Then the king arose very early in the morning and hurried to the lions' den. And when he came to the den, he cried with a grieved voice to Daniel. The king spoke and said to Daniel, O Daniel, servant of the living God, is your God whom you always serve able to deliver you from the lions?

Then Daniel said to the king, O king, live forever. My God has sent His angel and has shut the lions' mouths, and they have not hurt me, because before Him purity was found in me. And also, before you, O king, I have done no harm. Then the king was exceedingly glad for him and commanded that they should take Daniel up out of the den. So, Daniel was taken up out of the den, and no kind of hurt was found on him because he trusted in his God.

And the king commanded, and they brought those men who had accused Daniel, and they threw them into the lions' den; them, their sons, and their wives. And the lions overpowered them and broke all their bones in pieces before they came to the bottom of the den. Then King Darius wrote to all people, nations, and languages that dwell in all the earth. Peace is multiplied to you.

I make a decree that in all the domain of my kingdom there shall be trembling and fear before the God of Daniel. "For He is the living God and endures forever, and His kingdom

*is that which shall not be destroyed, and His rule shall be to
the end.*

(Dan 6:1-26)

The Fiery Furnace:

What God did for these his servants would help to
keep the Jews to their religion while in captivity, and to cure
them of idolatry. The miracle brought deep convictions on
Nebuchadnezzar. But no abiding change then took place in
his conduct. Know that He, who preserved these pious Jews
in the fiery furnace, is able to uphold us in the hour of
temptation, and to keep us from falling into sin. Then King
Nebuchadnezzar was filled with wrath, and the form of his
face was changed against Shadrach, Meshach, and
Abednego.

He spoke and commanded that they should heat the
furnace seven times more than it was usually heated. And he
commanded mighty men in his army to tie up Shadrach,
Meshach, and Abednego, and to throw them into the burning
fiery furnace.

Then these men were tied up in their slippers, their
tunics, and their mantles, and their other clothes, and was
thrown into the middle of the burning fiery furnace. Then
because the king's commandment was urgent, and the
furnace exceedingly hot, the flame of the fire killed those
men who took up Shadrach, Meshach, and Abednego. And
these three men, Shadrach, Meshach, and Abednego, fell
down bound into the midst of the burning fiery furnace.

Then Nebuchadnezzar the king was amazed. And he rose up in haste and spoke and said to his advisers, did we not throw three men bound into the middle of the fire? They answered and said to the king, True, O king. He answered and said, Behold! I see four men lose, walking in the middle of the fire, and there is no harm among them. And the form of the fourth is like a son of the gods. (Dan 3:19-25)

The best way to have a good night is to keep a good conscience. We are sure of what the king doubted that the servants of the living God have a Master well able to protect them. See the power of God over the fiercest creatures, and believe his power to restrain the roaring lion that goes about continually seeking to devour. Daniel was kept perfectly safe because he believed in his God.

Those who boldly and cheerfully trust in God to protect them in the way of duty shall always find him a present help. Thus, the righteous is delivered out of trouble, and the wicked cometh in his stead. The short triumph of the wicked will end in their ruin.

It is no new thing for what is done faithfully, in conscience toward God, to be misrepresented as done obstinately, and in contempt of the civil powers. Through want of due thought, we often do that which afterward, like Darius, we see cause thousand times to wish undone again. Daniel, that venerable man, is brought as the vilest of malefactors and is thrown into the den of lions, to be devoured, only for worshipping his God.

No doubt the placing the stone was ordered by the providence of God, that the miracle of Daniel's deliverance might appear plainer; and the king sealed it with his own signet, probably lest Daniel's enemies should kill him. Let us commit our lives and souls unto God, in well-doing. We cannot place full confidence even in men whom we faithfully serve; but believers may, in all cases, be sure of the Divine favor and consolation.

If we live in the fear of God and walk according to that rule, peace shall be upon us. The kingdom, the power, and the glory, forever, are the Lord's; but many are employed in making known his wonderful works to others, who themselves remain strangers to his saving grace. May we be doers, as well as believers of his word, least at the last we should be found to have deceived ourselves?

The Handwriting on the Wall:

Belshazzar bade defiance to the judgments of God. Most historians consider that Cyrus then besieged Babylon. Security and sensuality are sad proofs of approaching ruin. That mirth is sinful indeed, which profanes sacred things and what are many of the songs used at modern feasts better than the praises sung by the heathens to their gods now see how God struck a terror upon Belshazzar and his lords.

God's written word is enough to put the proudest, boldest sinner in a fright. What we see of God, the part of the hand that writes in the book of the creatures, and in the book of the Scriptures they should fill us with awful thoughts concerning that part which we do not see.

If this is the finger of God, what is his arm when made bare? And what is He? The king's guilty conscience told him that he had no reason to expect any good news from heaven. God can, in a moment, make the heart of the stoutest sinner to tremble; and there needs no more than to let loose his own thoughts upon him; they will give him trouble enough.

No one's bodily pain can equal the inward agony which sometimes seizes the sinner in the midst of mirth, carnal pleasures, and worldly pomp. Sometimes terrors cause a man to flee to Christ for pardon and peace; but many cries out for fear of wrath, who are not humbled for their sins, and who seek relief by lying vanities. The ignorance and uncertainty concerning the Holy Scriptures, shown by many who call themselves wise, only tend to drive sinners to despair, as the ignorance of these wise men did.

Belshazzar bade defiance to the judgments of God. Most historians consider that Cyrus then besieged Babylon. Security and sensuality are sad proofs of approaching ruin. That mirth is sinful indeed which profanes sacred things and what are many of the songs used at modern feasts better than the praises sung by the heathens to their gods and their football games.

See how God struck a terror upon Belshazzar and his lords. God's written word is enough to put the proudest, boldest sinner in a fright. What we see of God, the part of the hand that writes in the book of the creatures, and in the book of the Scriptures, should fill us with awful thoughts concerning that part which we do not see. If this is the finger of God, what is his arm when made bare? And what is He?

The king's guilty conscience told him that he had no reason to expect any good news from heaven. God can, in a moment, make the heart of the stoutest sinner to tremble; and there needs no more than to let loose his own thoughts upon him; they will give him trouble enough. No bodily pain can equal the inward agony which sometimes seizes the sinner in the midst of mirth, carnal pleasures, and worldly pomp. Sometimes terrors cause a man to flee to Christ for pardon and peace; but many cries out for fear of wrath, who are not humbled for their sins, and who seek relief by lying vanities.

The ignorance and uncertainty concerning the Holy Scriptures, shown by many who call themselves wise, only tend to drive sinners to despair, as the ignorance of these wise men did. "At that moment fingers of a man's hand came out and wrote on the plaster of the wall of the king's palace across from the lampstand. And the king saw the part of the hand that wrote.

Then the king's face was changed, and his thoughts troubled him so that the joints of his loins were loosened, and his knees knocked against one another. "The king cried aloud to bring in the conjurers, the Chaldeans, and the fortune-tellers. The king spoke and said to the wise men of Babylon, Whoever shall read this writing, and show me its meaning, shall be clothed with scarlet, and have a chain of gold around his neck, and shall be the third ruler in the kingdom.

Then all the king's wise men came in. But they could not read the writing, nor make the meaning known to the king. Then King Belshazzar was greatly troubled, and his face was changing in him, and his lords were perplexed. (Dan 5:6-9)

Daniel was forgotten at court; he lived privately and was then ninety years of age. Many consult servants of God on curious questions, or to explain difficult subjects, but without asking the way of salvation, or the path of duty.

Daniel slighted the offer of reward. He spoke to Belshazzar as to a condemned criminal. We should despise all the gifts and rewards this world can give, did we see, as we may by faith, its end hastening on; but let us do our duty in the world and do it all the real service we can "Oh king, the Highest God gave King Nebuchadnezzar your father a kingdom, and majesty, and glory, and honor. And for the majesty that He gave him, all people, nations, and languages trembled and feared before him. He killed whom he would, and whom he would he kept alive. And whom he would, he set up; and whom he would, he put down.

But when his heart was lifted up, and his mind hardened in pride, he was put down from the throne of his kingdom, and they took his glory from him. And he was driven from the sons of men. And his heart was made like the animals, and his dwelling was with the wild asses. They fed him with grass like oxen, and his body was wet with the dew of the heavens until he knew that the Highest God rules in the kingdom of men and that He appoints over it whomever He will.

"And you his son, O Belshazzar, have not humbled your heart, though you knew all this. But you have lifted up yourself against the Lord of Heaven. And they have brought the vessels of His house before you; and you, and your lords, your wives, and your concubines, have drunk wine from them. And you have praised the gods of silver, and gold, of bronze, iron, wood, and stone, which do not see, nor hear, nor know. And you have not glorified the God in whose hand is your breath and all your ways.

Then the part of the hand was sent from Him. And this writing was written. And this is the writing that was written, A MINA, A MINA, A SHEKEL, AND HALF-MINAS. This is the meaning of the thing: A MINA, God has numbered your kingdom and finished it. A SHEKEL, you are weighed in the balances and found wanting. HALF-MINAS, your kingdom is divided and given to the Medes and Persians.

Then Belshazzar commanded, and they clothed Daniel with scarlet and a golden chain around his neck and made a proclamation concerning him that he should be the third ruler in the kingdom. In that night Belshazzar the king of the Chaldeans was killed. And Darius the Mede took the kingdom, being a son of sixty-two years. (Dan 5:22-31)

Daniel reads Belshazzar's doom. He had not taken warning by the judgments upon Nebuchadnezzar. And he had insulted God.

Sinners are pleased with gods that neither see, nor hear, nor know, but they will be judged by One to whom all things are open. Daniel reads the sentence written on the wall. All this may well be applied to the doom of every sinner. At death, the sinner's days are numbered and finished; after death is the judgment, when he will be weighed in the balance, and found wanting; and after judgment, the sinner will be cut asunder, and given as a prey to the devil and his angels.

While these things were passing in the palace, it is considered that the army of Cyrus entered the city; and when Belshazzar was slain, a general submission followed. Soon will every impenitent sinner find the writing of God's word brought to pass upon him, whether he is weighed in the balance of the law as a self-righteous Pharisee, or in that of the gospel as a painted hypocrite?

We notice to the glory of God, that though Daniel was now very old, yet he was able for business, and had continued faithful to his religion. It is for the glory of God, when those who profess religion, conduct themselves so that their most watchful enemies may find no occasion for blaming them, save only in the matters of their God, in which they walk according to their consciences.

Daniel Prayer of Agreement with God:

"It pleased Darius to set over the kingdom a hundred and twenty satraps that they might be over the whole kingdom. And over them were three presidents (Daniel was one of them), so that these satraps might give account to them, and the king should have no loss. Then this Daniel was made overseer of the presidents and satraps because an excellent spirit was in him. And the king was planning to set him over the entire kingdom.

Then the presidents and rulers sought to find occasion against Daniel concerning the kingdom. But they could find no occasion or fault because he was faithful. Neither was there any error or fault found in him. Then these men said we shall not find any occasion against this Daniel unless we find it against him concerning the Law of his God.

Then these presidents and rulers assembled to the king and said this to him: King Darius, live forever. All the presidents of the kingdom, the prefects, and the satraps, and the officials and governors, have planned together to establish a royal law, and to make a strong ban that whoever shall ask a petition of any god or man for thirty days, except from you, O king; he shall be thrown into the den of lions.

Now, O king, establish the ban and sign the writing, so that it may not be changed, according to the law of the Medes and Persians which cannot be changed. Therefore, King Darius signed the writing and the ban. And when he had learned that the document was signed, Daniel went to his house. And his windows were open in his roof room toward Jerusalem; and he kneeled on his knees three times a day and prayed, and gave thanks before his God, as he did before.

To forbid prayer for thirty days is, for so long, to rob God of all the tribute he has from man, and to rob the man of all the comfort he has in God. Does not every man's heart direct him, when in want or distress, to call upon God? We could not live a day without God; and can men live thirty days without prayer?

Yet it is to be feared that those who, without any decree forbidding them, present no hearty, serious petitions to God for more than thirty days together, are far more numerous than those who serve him continually, with humble, thankful hearts. Persecuting laws are always made on false pretenses, but it does not become Christians to make bitter complaints or to indulge in reviling. It is good to have hours for prayer. Daniel prayed openly and avowedly; and though a man of vast business, he did not think that would excuse him from daily exercises of devotion.

How inexcusable are those who have but little to do in the world, yet will not do this much for their souls! In trying times, we must take heed, lest, under the pretense of discretion, we are guilty of cowardice in the cause of God. All who throw away their souls, as those certainly do that live without prayer, even if it be to save their lives, at the end will be found to be fools.

Nor did Daniel only pray, and not give thanks, cutting off some part of the service to make the time of danger shorter; but he performed the whole. In a word, the duty of prayer is founded upon the sufficiency of God as an almighty Creator and Redeemer, and upon our wants as sinful creatures. To Christ, we must turn our eyes.

Let nothing be done through strife or vainglory, but in lowliness of mind let each esteem other better than themselves. Do not let each man look upon his own things, but each man also on the things of others. For let this mind be in you which was also in Christ Jesus, who, being in the form of God, thought it not robbery to be equal with God,
(Philippians 2:3-6)

Here are further exhortations to Christian duties; to like-mindedness and lowly-mindedness, according to the example of the Lord Jesus. Kindness is the law of Christ's kingdom, the lesson of his school, the livery of his family. Several motives to brotherly love are mentioned. If you expect or experience the benefit of God's compassions to yourselves, be compassionate one to another.

It is the joy of ministers to see people like-minded. Christ came to humble us, let there not be among us a spirit of pride. We must be severe upon our own faults, and quick in observing our own defects, but ready to make favorable allowances for others. We must kindly care for others, but not be busy-bodies in other men's matters. Neither inward nor outward peace can be enjoyed, without lowliness of mind.

It is no new thing for what is done faithfully, in conscience toward God, to be misrepresented as done obstinately, and in contempt of the civil powers. Through want of due thought, we often do that which afterward, like Darius, we see cause thousand times to wish undone again. Daniel, that venerable man, is brought as the vilest of malefactors and is thrown into the den of lions, to be devoured, only for worshipping his God.

No doubt the placing the stone was ordered by the providence of God, that the miracle of Daniel's deliverance might appear plainer; and the king sealed it with his own signet, probably lest Daniel's enemies should kill him. Let us commit our lives and souls unto God, in well-doing. We cannot place full confidence even in men whom we faithfully serve; but believers may, in all cases, be sure of the Divine favor and consolation.

Chapter 4

Daniel Vision

"In the first year of Belshazzar king of Babylon, Daniel had a dream and visions of his head on his bed. Then he wrote the dream and gave the sum of the matters. Daniel spoke and said, in my vision by night I was looking: and behold, the four winds of the heavens were stirring up the Great Sea.

He first was like a lion and had eagle's wings. I watched until its wings were plucked, and it was lifted up from the earth and made to stand on its feet like a man. And a man's heart was given to it. And behold another beast, a second, like a bear. And it raised itself up on one side, and it had three ribs in its mouth between its teeth.

And they said this to it: Arise, eat up much flesh. After this, I saw, and lo, another, like a leopard, which had four, wings of a bird on its back. The beast also had four heads, and rulership was given to it. The beast also had four heads, and rulership was given to it. After this, I looked in the night visions, and behold, a fourth beast, frightening and terrifying, and very strong. And it had great iron teeth; it devoured and broke in pieces and stamped the rest with its feet.

And it was different from all the beasts before it, and it had ten horns. I was thinking about the horns, and behold, there came up among them another little horn, before which three of the first horns were uprooted. And behold, in this horn were eyes like the eyes of man, and a mouth speaking great things.

Know that his vision contains the same prophetic representations with Nebuchadnezzar's dream. The great sea agitated by the winds, represented the earth and the dwellers on it troubled by ambitious princes and conquerors. The four beasts signified the same four empires, as the four parts of Nebuchadnezzar's image.

Mighty conquerors are but instruments of God's vengeance on a guilty world. The savage beast represents the hateful features of their characters. But the dominion given to each has a limit; their wrath shall be made to praise the Lord, and the remainder of it he will restrain.

Ancient Days and Interpretation of the Four Beasts:

"I watched until the thrones were set in place, and the Ancient of Days sat, whose robe was white as snow, and the hair of His head like the pure wool. His throne was like flames of fire, and His wheels like burning fire. A stream of fire went out and came out from before Him. A thousand served Him, and ten thousand times ten thousand stood before Him. The judgment was set, and the books were opened.

Then I was looking because of the voice of the great words which the horn spoke. I watched until the beast was slain, and his body was destroyed and given to the burning flame. And the rest of the beasts, their dominion was taken away. Yet their lives were made longer for a season and time. I saw in the night visions, and behold, one like the Son of man came with the clouds of heaven and came to the Ancient of Days, and they brought Him near before Him. And dominion and glory were given Him, and a kingdom, that all peoples, nations, and languages, should serve Him. His dominion is an everlasting dominion which shall not pass away, and His kingdom that which shall not be destroyed.

These verses are for the comfort and support of the people of God, in reference to the persecutions that would come upon them. Many New Testament predictions of the judgment to come have a plain allusion to this vision; especially the book Rev.20:11, Rev. 20:12. The Messiah is here called the Son of man; he was made in the likeness of sinful flesh and was found in fashion as a man, but he is the Son of God.

The great event foretold in this passage, is Christ's glorious coming, to destroy every antichristian power, and to render his own kingdom universal upon the earth. But ere the solemn time arrives, for manifesting the glory of God to all worlds in his dealings with his creatures, we may expect that the doom of each of us will be determined at the hour of our death; and before the end shall come, the Father will openly give to his incarnate Son, our Mediator, and Judge, the inheritance of the nations as his willing subjects.

It is desirable to obtain the right and full sense of what we see and hear from God, and those that would know must ask by faithful and fervent prayer. The angel told Daniel plainly. He especially desired to know respecting the little horn, which made war with the saints and prevailed against them.

Here is foretold the rage of papal Rome against true Christians. St. John, in his visions and prophecies, which point in the first place in Rome, has a plain reference to these visions. Daniel had a joyful prospect of the prevalence of God's kingdom among men. This refers to the second coming of our blessed Lord when the saints shall triumph in the complete fall of Satan's kingdom.

The saints of the Highest shall possess the kingdom forever. Far be it from us to infer from hence, that dominion is founded on grace.

It promises that the gospel kingdom shall be set up; a kingdom of light, holiness, and love; a kingdom of grace, the privileges, and comforts of which shall be the earnest and first-fruits of the kingdom of glory. But the full accomplishment will be in the everlasting happiness of the saints, the kingdom that cannot be moved. The gathering together the whole family of God will be a blessedness of Christ's coming.

<u>The Ram and the Male Goat:</u>

God gives Daniel a foresight of seeing the destruction of other kingdoms, which in their day were as powerful as that of Babylon. Could we foresee the changes that shall be when we are gone, we should be less affected with changes in our own day? The ram with two horns was the second empire, that of Media and Persia. He saw this ram overcome by a he-goat.

This was Alexander the Great. Alexander, when about thirty-three years of age, and in his full strength, died, and showed the vanity of worldly pomp and power, and that they cannot make a man happy. While men dispute, as in the case of Alexander, respecting the death of some prosperous warrior, it is plain that the great First Cause of all had no more of his plan for him to execute, and therefore cut him off. Instead of that one great horn, there came up four notable ones, Alexander's four chief captains. A little horn became a great persecutor of the church and people of God.

It seems that the Mohammedan delusion is here pointed out. It prospered, and at one time nearly destroyed the holy religion God's right hand had planted. It is just with God to deprive those of the privileges of his house who despise and profane them; and to make those know the worth of ordinances by the want of them, who would not know it by the enjoyment of them.

Daniel heard the time of this calamity limited and determined; but not the time when it should come. If we would know the mind of God, we must apply to Christ, in whom are hid all the treasures of wisdom and knowledge; not hid from us, but hid for us. There is much difficulty as to the precise time here stated, but the end of it cannot be very distant. God will, for his own glory, see to the cleansing of the church in due time. Christ died to cleanse his church, and he will so cleanse it as to present it blameless to himself.

In the third year of the reign of king Belshazzar a vision appeared to me, to me, Daniel, after that which appeared to me at the first. And in a vision, I looked. And it happened when I looked I was at Shushan the palace, which is in the province of Elam. And in a vision, I looked, and I was by the Ulai Canal.

Then I lifted up my eyes and looked. And behold, a ram with two horns stood before the canal having two horns, and the two horns were high, but one was higher than the other, and the higher came up last. I saw the ram pushing westward and northward and southward; so that no beasts could stand before him or any that could deliver out of his hand.

But he did according to his will and became great. And as I was watching behold he goat came from the west over the face of all earth and did not touch the ground. And he-goat had an outstanding horn between his eyes. And he came to the ram that had two horns, which I had seen standing before the river, and ran to him in the fury of his power. (Dan 8:1-6) The eternal Son of God stood before the prophet in the appearance of a man and directed the angel Gabriel to explain the vision. Daniel's fainting and astonishment at the prospect of evils he saw coming on his people and the church, confirm the opinion that long-continued calamities were foretold.

The vision being ended, a charge was given to Daniel to keep it private for the present. He kept it to himself and went on to do the duty of his place. As long as we live in this world we must have something to do in it; and even those whom God has most honored, must not think themselves above their business. Nor must the pleasure of communion with God take us from the duties of our callings, but we must in them abide with God.

All who are intrusted with public business must discharge their trust uprightly; and, amidst all doubts and discouragements, they may, if true believers look forward to a happy issue. Thus, should we Endeavour to compose our minds for attending to the duties to which each is appointed, in the church and in the world?

Chapter 5

The Vision of the Scriptures of Truth

The angel shows Daniel the succession of the Persian and Grecian empires. The kings of Egypt and Syria are noticed: Judea was between their dominions and affected by their contests. From vs. 5-30, is generally considered to relate to the events which came to pass during the continuance of these governments; and from Dan. 11:21, to relate to Antiochus Epiphanies, who was a cruel and violent persecutor of the Jews.

See what decaying, perishing things worldly pomp and possessions are, and the power by which they are gotten. God, in His providence, sets up one, and pulls down another, as he pleases. This world is full of wars and fighting's, which come from men's lusts. All changes and revolutions of states and kingdoms and every event are plainly and perfectly foreseen by God.

No word of God shall fall to the ground; but what he has designed, what he has declared, shall infallibly come to pass. While the potsherds of the earth strive with each other, they prevail and are prevailed against, deceive and are deceived; but those who know God will trust in him, and he will enable them to stand their ground, bear their cross, and maintain their conflict.

The remainder of this prophecy is very difficult, and commentators differ much respecting it. From Antiochus, the account seems to pass to antichrist. The reference seems to be made to the Roman Empire, the fourth monarchy, in its pagan, early Christian, and the Papal States.

The end of the Lord's anger against his people approaches, as well as the end of his patience towards his enemies. If we would escape the ruin of the infidel, the idolater, the superstitious and cruel persecutor, as well as that of the profane, let us make the oracles of God our standard of truth and of duty, the foundation of our hope, and the light of our paths through this dark world, to the glorious inheritance above.

The conclusion of the vision of the Scriptures of truth Michael signifies, "Who is like God" and his name with the title of the great Prince" points out the Divine Savior. Christ stood for the children of our people in their stead as a sacrifice, bore the curse for them, to bear it from them. He stands for them in pleading for them at the throne of grace. And after the destruction of antichrist, the Lord Jesus shall stand at the latter day upon the earth; and He shall appear for the complete redemption of all his people.

When God works deliverance for us from persecution for them, it is as life from the dead. When his gospel is preached, many who sleep in the dust, both Jews and Gentiles, shall be awakened by it out of their heathenism of Judaism. And in the end the multitude that sleeps in the dust shall awake; many shall arise to life, and many to shame. There is glory reserved for all the saints in the future state, for all that are wise, wise for their souls and eternity.

Those who turn many to righteousness, who turn sinners from the errors of their ways, and help to save their souls from death, Jam. 5:20 will share in the glory of those they have helped to heaven, which will add to their own glory. The times of the continuance of these events will come.

One of the angels asking how long it should be to the end of these wonders, a solemn reply is made, that it would be for a time, times, and a half, the period mentioned Dan. 7:25, and in Revelation. It signifies 1260 prophetic days or years, beginning from the time when the power of the holy people should be scattered. The imposture of Mohammed and the papal usurpation began about the same time, and these were a twofold attack upon the church of God. But all will end well at last.

All opposing rule, principality, and power shall be put down, and holiness and love will triumph, and be in honor, to eternity. The end, this end, shall come. What an amazing prophecy is this, of so many varied events, and extending through so many successive ages, even to the general resurrection! Daniel must comfort himself with the pleasing prospect of his own happiness in death, in judgment, and to eternity.

It is good for us all to think much about going away from this world. That must be our way; but it is our comfort that we shall not go till God calls us to another world, and till he has done with us in this world; till he says, go thou thy way, thou hast done thy work, therefore now, go thy way, and leave it to others to take thy place.

It was a comfort to Daniel, and is a comfort to all the saints, that whatever their lot is in the days of their lives, they shall have a happy lot at the end of the days. And it ought to be the great care and concern of every one of us to secure this. Then we may well be content with our present lot and welcome the will of God. Believers are happy at all times; they rest in God by faith now, and a rest is reserved for them in heaven at last.

Apologetics:

In all of the world's literature apart from the Bible, there is no prophecy that correctly specifies the nature and timing of unusual events hundreds of years in the future. Yet the prophecy laid out in Daniel 9:25-26, written centuries before the time of Jesus, yields specific dates for several key events in His ministry. Thus, this prophecy is in itself enough to establish, first, that the Bible is the Word of God and, secondly, that the one who came at the appointed time was the promised Messiah.

Oracle of Daniel:

The remarkable prophecy concerning the time of Christ's coming is known as the prophecy of sixty-nine weeks. Seventy weeks are determined upon thy people and upon thy holy city, to finish the transgression, and to make an end of sins, and to make reconciliation for iniquity, and to bring in everlasting righteousness, and to seal up the vision and prophecy, and to anoint the holiest.

Know therefore and understand, that from the going forth of the commandment to restore and to build Jerusalem unto the Messiah the Prince shall be seven weeks, and threescore and two weeks: the street shall be built again, and the wall, even in troublous times. Daniel 9:24-25The Old Testament book containing this prophecy was written by Daniel, a Jewish captive of the Babylonians who became a high official of both Babylonia and Persia during the sixth century BC.

In chapter 9, Daniel records that after he pleaded with God to turn His wrath away from the Jewish people, God sent him a prophetic message through the angel Gabriel. This prophecy is perhaps the most astounding in a book full of astounding prophecies. Hundreds of years before the event, the Lord foretold through Daniel exactly when the Messiah would come. Christian apologists of the past have proposed many solutions for Daniel's prophecy of the sixty-nine weeks, but none except the one presented here rely upon a defensible scheme of dates (1).

Mention of "the street" in Daniel 9:25, therefore, exclude any work on the city before Nehemiah became governor. Although the exiles who returned in the days of Cyrus had in some measure restored the city and its wall (Ezra 4:12), Nehemiah's report on the condition of the city leaves little doubt that at the time of his coming, the Water Gate had not yet been reclaimed for use.

2. To confirm that it is referring to the work done under Nehemiah, the prophecy adds that the rebuilding of the city would take place "even in troublous times." Indeed, fearing an attack by hostile neighbors, the workers wore or carried weapons (Neh. 4:17).

As you stand to rebuild the wall it is important to watch always against spiritual enemies, and not expect that our warfare will be over till our work is ended. The word of God is the sword of the Spirit, which we ought to have always at hand, and never to have to look for it, either in our labors or in our conflicts, as Christians. The word of God should be a way of life to the true believer.

Summer of Daniel:

Today in our time we have people God has chosen that are passing through time with Daniel ability that has strong faith in God Daniel had when he went into the lion's den. We all know that prayer changes things but prayer without faith and trust the den of lions will have you for dinner. God talks to us in his word, therefore, we must know the word of God and pray the word of God and when we can do this with faith and trust then we will have the den of lions for dinner.

Daniel was strong in his belief and had a real relationship with God and to show his obedience to God he purposed in his heart to not defile himself by eating the King meat. What would you purposed in his heart daily to not defile your walk with God? Will you walk in love, in God's Spirit or will you walk upright for God in all that you do? Think about it.

I purposed in the heart never to walk in my own rightness but to always walk in the rightness of God that is a daily prayer for me. We must prove our self to God by taking on his gift of love and walk in love daily. The gift of love is the one thing we should master in our walk with God. Love is a spiritual gift that is rarely sought after and yet God is love.

When we are babes in Christ we never thought to ask God to give us wisdom and knowledge so we walk through our Christin experience never getting the understanding of what wisdom and knowledge really would mean to our experience with God.

There are some that do get it and there are some that never get it and as an intercessor, I try to be mindful when I pray for others that God would grant them the wisdom and knowledge of who he really is so that in their journey through the time they will find God. God gave Daniel and his three friends wisdom and knowledge and I know that through prayer he will give it to the ones that I pray for as well. God gives wisdom to the wise and knowledge to them that know to understand.

What I took to heart in the Book of Daniel was the lesson of King Nebuchadnezzar and his experience of disobedience; it made it very clear to me that it is better to follow the command or guidance of God even if I had the power to do as I wish in my own flesh.

What King Nebuchadnezzar was not willing to understand was that Daniel's God was all-powerful, all-knowing and he was the only one that could do as he, please. King Nebuchadnezzar helped to me understand clearly that disobedience do product action that will make wish you had obeyed.

Daniel was a seer who has an open vision and Daniel also had the gift of prophetic dreams he was God chosen Prophet doing his times, a prophetic intercessor and God use Daniel to write prophecy and interprets Dreams.

For years I knew that I was a Prophetess and that I was a person that has an open prophetic vision, prophetic dreams, and a prophetic intercessor and when lead by God I write prophecy and interpret Dreams but I had never had the revelation until writing this book that I walked in all of Daniel gifts.

To everything, there is a season and a time to every purpose under the heaven and we never know just when it is our time until God tells you it's your time. I am sure when

Daniel started the journey he had no idea that God would use him in this grate way. To me, Daniel faith and trust in God is the greatest example to follow God for all times.

About the Author

Dr. Warren the publish Author, Chaplain and God's Prophetess. As a dedicated Intercessor, she is respected as a woman of prayer throughout her family, friends and Ministries associates. Dr. Warren is a wife and mother.

Dr. Warren is forever grateful to God for the journey of teaching her excellence in the Ministry of Prayer. Her Love for God has granted her wisdom and foresight; the comforts of his Love, the joy of his presence, the influence of his Spirit, and the enjoyment of his Ministry.

She is thankful that out of love the FATHER gave his SON and out of Love the SON gave his LIFE and out of love she took up her cross and follows HIM.

Dr. Warren Prayer for You

I thank my God through Jesus Christ for you all, that your faith is spoken of throughout the whole world. For God is my witness, whom I serve with my spirit and whole heart in the gospel of his Son Jesus, that without ceasing I make mention of you always in my prayers, my prayer request if by any means at length I may have a prosperous journey by the will of God to come to you. For I long to see you, that I may impart to you some spiritual gift, to the end that you may be established.

That is, that I may be comforted together with you, by the Holy Spirit and faith both of you and me. For I am not ashamed of the gospel of Christ: for it is the power of God to salvation to everyone that believeth. For in this is the righteousness of God revealed from faith to faith: as it is written, the just shall live by faith. Even so then at this present time may we be the remnant according to the election of grace.

Now may the God of hope fill you with all joy and peace in believing, that you may abound in hope, through the power of the Holy Spirit and that God's Grace will overpower you in all that you do and grant you wisdom, knowledge, revelation and most of all understanding of Him and who God truly is.

Dr. Emma T. Warren, Chaplain

Bibliography

James Orr M.A., D.D. General Editor, International Standard Bible Encyclopedia, Matthew Henry's Commentary On the whole Bible Publishers, Hendrickson, the Nelson's Illustrated Bible Dictionary Thomas Nelson Publishers 1968, Old Testament Survey Second Edition William B. Eerdmans Publishing Company First Edition 1982, Second Edition 1996.

Appendix

Daniel

(1) One of the sons of David (1Ch 3:1).

(2) A Levite of the family of Ithamar (Ezr 8:2; Neh 10:6).

(3) A prophet of the time of Nebuchadnezzar and Cyrus, the hero and author of the Book of Daniel.

Darius

(1) Darius the Mede (Dan 6:1; Dan 11:1) was the son of *Ahasuerus* (Xerxes) of the seed of the Medes (Dan 9:1). He received the government of Belshazzar the Chaldean upon the death of that prince (Dan 5:30, Dan 5:31; Dan 6:1), and was made a king over the kingdom of the Chaldeans.

From Dan 6:28 we may infer that Darius was king contemporaneously with Cyrus. Outside of the Book of Daniel there is no mention of Darius the Mede by name, though there are good reasons for identifying him with Subaru, or Ugbaru, the governor of Gutium, who is said in the Nabunaid-Cyrus Chronicle to have been appointed by Cyrus as his governor of Babylon after its capture from the Chaldeans.

Dethroned by seven Persian nobles from among whom Darius was selected to be king. After many rebellions and wars, he succeeded in establishing himself firmly upon the throne (*Ant.*, XI, i). He reorganized and enlarged the Persian Empire. He is best known to general history from his conflict with Greece culminating at Marathon, and for his re-digging of the Suez Canal. In sacred history, he stands forth as the king who enabled the Jews under Joshua and Zerubbabel to rebuild the temple at Jerusalem.

(3) Darius, called by the Greeks No Thus, was called Ochus before he became king. He reigned from 424 to 404 bc. In the Scriptures he is mentioned only in Neh 12:22, where he is called Darius the Persian, probably to distinguish him from Darius the Mede.

Nebuchadnezzar.

The Babylonian name given to Daniel (Dan 1:7; Dan 2:26; Dan 5:12). Not to be confounded with Belshazzar

His name is found in two forms in the Bible, Nebuchadnezzar, and Nebuchadnezzar. In the Septuagint, he is called Ναβουχοδονοσόρ, *Nabouchodonosór*, and in the Vulgate (Jerome's Latin Bible, 390-405 A.D.) *Nabuchodonosor*. This latter form is found also in the King James Version Apocrypha throughout and in the Revised Version (British and American) 1 Esdras, Ad Esther and Baruch, but not Judith or Tobit.

This change from "r" to "n" which is found in the two writings of the name in the Hebrew and the Aramaic of the Scriptures is a not uncommon one in the Semitic languages, as in Burnaburiyash and Burraburiyash, Ben-had ad and Bar-Hadad (see Brockelmann's *Comparative Grammar*, 136, 173, 220). It is possible, however, that the form Nebuchadnezzar is the Aramaic translation of the Babylonian Nebuchadrezzar.

2. Family:

The father of the King Nebuchadnezzar was Nabopolassar, probably a Chaldean prince. His mother is not known by name. The classical historians mention two wives: Amytis, the daughter of Astyages, and Nitocris, the mother of Nabunaid.

The monuments mention three sons: Evil-Merodach who succeeded him, Marduk-Shum-user, and Marduk-Nadin-achi. A younger brother of Nebuchadnezzar, called Nabu-Shum-lishir, is mentioned on a building-inscription tablet from the time of Nabopolassar.

3. Sources of Information:

The sources of our information as to the life of Nebuchadnezzar are about 500 contract tablets dated according to the days, months and years of his reign of 43 years; about 30 building and honorific inscriptions; one historical inscription; and in the books of Jeremiah, Ezekiel, Daniel, and Kings.

Later sources are Chronicles, Ezra, and the fragments of Berosus, Menander, Megasthenes, Abydenus, and Alexander Polyhistor, largely as cited by Josephus and Eusebius.

4. Political History:

From these sources, we learn that Nebuchadnezzar succeeded his father on the throne of Babylon in 604 BC, and reigned till 561 BC. He probably commanded the armies of Babylon from 609. BC. At any rate, he was at the head of the army which defeated Pharaoh-necoh at Carchemish on the

Euphrates in 605 BC (see 2Ki 23:31; 2Ch 35:20 ff).

After having driven Necoh out of Asia and settled the affairs of Syria and Palestine, he was suddenly recalled to Babylon by the death of his father. There he seems quiet to have ascended the throne.

In the 4th year of Jehoiakim (or 3rd according to the Babylonian manner of reckoning (Dan 1:1)), he came up first against Jerusalem and carried away part of the vessels of the temple and a few captives of noble lineage.

5. Buildings, Etc.:

The monuments justify the boast of Nebuchadnezzar "Is not this great Babylon that I have built?" (Dan 4:30). Among these buildings, special emphasis is placed by Nebuchadnezzar upon his temples and shrines to the gods, particularly to Marduk, Nebo, and Zarpinat, but also to Shamash, Sin, Gula, Ramman, Mah, and others. He constructed, also, a great new palace and rebuilt an old one of his father's. Besides, he laid out and paved with bricks a great street for the procession of Marduk, and built a number of great walls with moats and moat-walls and gates.

He dug several broad, deep canals, and made dams for flooding the country to the North and South of Babylon, so as to protect it against the attack of its enemies. He made, also, great bronze bulls and serpents, and adorned his temples and palaces with cedars and gold. Not merely in Babylon itself, but in many of the cities of Babylonia as well, his building operations were carried on, especially in the line of temples to the gods.

6. Religion, Etc.:

The inscriptions of Nebuchadnezzar show that he was a very religious man, probably excelling all who had preceded him in the building of temples, in the institution of offerings, and the observance of all the ceremonies connected with the worship of the gods.

His larger inscriptions usually contain two hymns and always close with a prayer. Mention is frequently made of the offerings of precious metals, stones, and woods, of game, fish, wine, fruit, grain, and other objects acceptable to the gods. It is worthy of note that these offerings differ in character and apparently in purpose from those in use among the Jews. For example, no mention is made in any one of Nebuchadnezzar's inscriptions of the pouring out or sprinkling of blood, nor is any reference made to atonement, or to sin.

7. Madness:

No reference is made in any of these inscriptions to Nebuchadnezzar's insanity. But aside from the fact that we could scarcely expect a man to publish his own calamity, especially madness, it should be noted that according to Langdon we have but three inscriptions of his written in the period from 580 to 561 BC.

If his madness lasted for 7 years, it may have occurred between 580 and 567 BC, or it may have occurred between the Egyptian campaign of 567 BC and his death in 561 BC. But, as it is more likely that the "7 times" mentioned in Dan may have been months, the illness may have been in any year after 580 BC, or even before that for all we know.

8. Miracles, Etc.:

No mention is made on the monuments (1) of the dream of Nebuchadnezzar recorded in Dan 2, or (2) of the image of gold that he set up, or (3) of the fiery furnace from which the three children were delivered (Dan 3). As to (1), it may be said, however, that a belief in dreams was so universal among all the ancient peoples, that a single instance of this kind may not have been considered as worthy of special mention. Jerusalem disproves them. The fact is, we have no real historical inscription of Nebuchadnezzar, except one fragment of a few broken lines found in Egypt.

Literature.

T.G. Pinches, *The New Testament in the Light of the Historical Records and Legends of Assyria and Babylonia*; Stephen Langdon, *Building Inscriptions of the Neo-Babylonian Empire*. See also, Rogers, *History of Babylonia and Assyria*; and McCurdy, *History, Prophecy and the Monuments*, III.

Meshach

mē´shak (מֵישַׁךְ, *meshakh*): Possibly the Sumerian form of the Babylonian *Ṣil-Asharidu*, "the shadow of the prince," just as Shadrach probably means "the servant of Sin," and Abednego the "servant of Ishtar." Meshach was one of the three Hebrew companions of Daniel, whose history is given in the first chapters of the Book of Daniel. See, further, under SHADRACH.

Mishael

mish´ā̆-el, mī´shā̆-el (מִישָׁאֵל, *mīshā'ēl*, perhaps = "who is equal to God?"):

(1) A Kohathite, 4th in descent from Levi (Exo_6:22). He and his brother Elzaphan carried out Moses' order to remove from the sanctuary and the camp the corpses of Nadab and Abihu (Lev_10:4 f).

(2) A supporter of Ezra at the reading of the Law (Neh_8:4).

(3) The Hebrew name of one of Daniel's 3 companions (Dan_1:6, Dan_1:7, Dan_1:11, Dan_1:19; Dan_2:17). His Babylonian name was MESHACH (which see).

Azariah

az-a-rī´a עֲזַרְיָהוּ, *'ăzaryāhū* and עֲזַרְיָה, *'ăzaryāh*, "Yahweh has helped"):

(1) King of Judah. See UZZIAH.

(2) A Judahite of the house of Ethan the Wise (1Ch_2:8).

(3) The son of Jehu descended from an Egyptian through the daughter of Sheshan (1Ch_2:38).

(4) A son of Ahimaaz and grandson of Zadok (1Ch 6:9).

(5) A son of Zadok the high priest and an official of Solomon (1Ki 4:2).

(6) A high priest and son of Johanan (1Ch 6:10).

(7) A Levite, ancestor of Samuel, and Heman the singer (1Ch 6:36).

(8) A son of Nathan and captain of Solomon's tax collectors (1Ki 4:5).

(9) A prophet in the reign of King Asa; his father's name was Oded (2Ch 15:1-8).

(10 and 11) Two sons of Jehoshaphat, king of Judah (2Ch 21:2).

(12) King of Judah (2Ch 22:6, called Ahaziah in 2Ch 22:1).

(13) A son of Jeroham, who helped to overthrow Athaliah, and place Joash on the throne (2Ch 23:1).

(14) A son of Johanan and a leading man of Ephraim mentioned in connection with the emancipated captives taken by Pekah (2Ch 28:12).

(15) A Levite of the family of Merari, who took part in cleansing the temple in the days of Hezekiah (2Ch_29:12).

(16) A high priest who rebuked King Uzziah for arrogating to himself priestly functions (2Ch_26:16-20).

(17) The father of Seraiah and son of Hilkiah (1Ch_6:13 f).

(18) A son of Hoshaiah, and a bitter enemy of Jeremiah (Jer_43:2).

(19) One of the royal captives taken to Babylon, whose name was changed to Abed-nego (Dan_1:7).

(20) The son of Maaseiah, who helped repair the walls of Jerusalem (Neh_3:23 f).

(21) A Levite who assisted Ezra to expound the Law (Neh_8:7).

(22) A priest who sealed the covenant (Neh_10:2).

(23) A prince of Judah mentioned in connection with the dedication of the walls of Jerusalem (Neh_12:32 f).

Suggested Books for Business

ARCO OFFICE GUIDE TO

Business English
Letters, Memos, and Reports
Business Math
Spelling & Word Division

HOW TO SAY IT

Choice Words, Phrases, Sentences
And Paragraphs for Every Situation
 Rosalie Maggio

Professional Secretary's Encyclopedic Dictionary

Mary A. De Vries

DICTIONARY OF BUSINESS TERMS
Jack P. Friedman

DICTIONARY OF BANKING TERMS

Thomas P. Fitch

GOD IS MY CEO

Larry Julian

SPIRITUAL SUGGESTED READING AND DVD LIST

David Barton
Wall Builders
PO Box 397
Aledo, TX 76008
1-800-873-2845

Books

Holiness, Truth and the Presence of God
Francis Frangipane

Arrow Publications
PO Box 10102
Cedar Rapids, IA 52410
319-395-7833

Love the Way to Victory
Kenneth E. Hagan
Kenneth Hagan Ministries
PO Box 50126
Tulsa, OK 74150-0126

The Power of Agreement
Pastor Rick Hawkins
PO Box 28402
San Antonio, TX 78228
210-432-5775

Scripture Keys for Kingdom Living
June Newman
Scripture Keys Ministries
PO Box 6559
Denver, Colorado 80206-0559

DANIEL the MAN of GOD

Dr. Emma T. Warren, Chaplain

Purchase Order

SHIP TO:
Please Print

Purchase Order #:
Date:
Vendor ID:

Your Name: _____

Address: _____

Email: _____

QUANTITY		DESCRIPTION		UNIT PRICE	TOTAL
		DANIEL the MAN of GOD		$10.00	$10.00
				Subtotal	
				Your Tax	
				Shipping	$4.00
Mail To:				Balance Due	

Dr. Emma T. Warren
2260 Ferdon Blvd Suite 110
Crestview FL 32536

Fax: To: 1-888-612-7721

DANIEL the MAN of GOD

Dr. Emma T. Warren, Chaplain

Purchase Order

SHIP TO:
Please Print

Purchase Order #:
Date:
Vendor ID:

Your Name: _____

Address: _____

Email: _____

QUANTITY		DESCRIPTION		UNIT PRICE	TOTAL
		DANIEL the MAN of GOD		$10.00	$10.00
				Subtotal	
				Your Tax	
				Shipping	$4.00
Mail To:				Balance Due	

Dr. Emma T. Warren
2260 Ferdon Blvd Suite 110
Crestview FL 32536

Fax: To: 1-888-612-7721

DANIEL the MAN of GOD

Dr. Emma T. Warren, Chaplain

Purchase Order

SHIP TO:
Please Print

Purchase Order #:
Date:
Vendor ID:

Your Name: _____

Address: _____

Email: _____

QUANTITY		DESCRIPTION		UNIT PRICE	TOTAL
		DANIEL the MAN of GOD		$10.00	$10.00
			Subtotal		
			Your Tax		
			Shipping		$4.00
Mail To:				Balance Due	

Dr. Emma T. Warren
2260 Ferdon Blvd Suite 110
Crestview FL 32536

Fax: To: 1-888-612-7721

DANIEL the MAN of GOD

Dr. Emma T. Warren, Chaplain

Purchase Order

SHIP TO:
Please Print

Purchase Order #:
Date:
Vendor ID:

Your Name: _____

Address: _____

Email: _____

QUANTITY		DESCRIPTION		UNIT PRICE	TOTAL
		DANIEL the MAN of GOD		$10.00	$10.00
				Subtotal	
				Your Tax	
				Shipping	$4.00
Mail To:				Balance Due	

Dr. Emma T. Warren
2260 Ferdon Blvd Suite 110
Crestview FL 32536

Fax: To: 1-888-612-7721

DRETWC... DANIEL the MAN of GOD |

DANIEL the MAN of GOD

Dr. Emma T. Warren, Chaplain

Purchase Order

SHIP TO:
Please Print

Purchase Order #:
Date:
Vendor ID:

Your Name: _____

Address: _____

Email: _____

QUANTITY		DESCRIPTION		UNIT PRICE	TOTAL
		DANIEL the MAN of GOD		$10.00	$10.00
				Subtotal	
				Your Tax	
				Shipping	$4.00
Mail To:				Balance Due	

Dr. Emma T. Warren
2260 Ferdon Blvd Suite 110
Crestview FL 32536

Fax: To: 1-888-612-7721

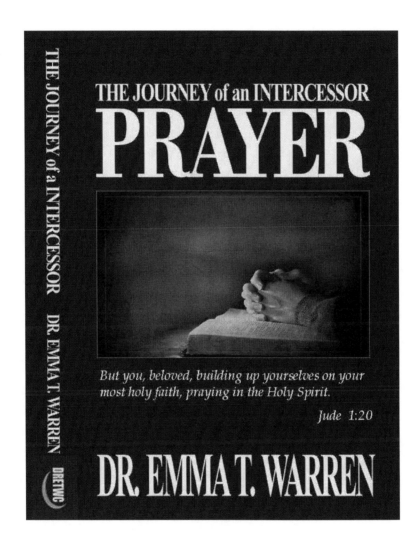

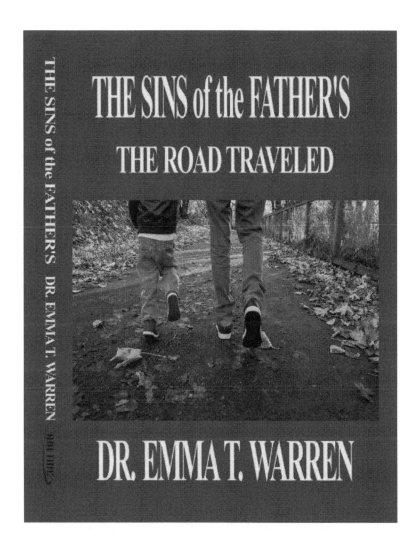

2260 South Fredon Blvd Suite 110
Crestview FL 32536

http://www. thompsonwarrenfoundation.com
Email DRETWC.T@gmail.com

800 # 888-488-8550
Fax: 888-612-7721

NOTES

NOTES

NOTES

NOTES

NOTES

-END-